JULIUS CAESAR
ROMAN LEADER

Christine Dugan, M.A.Ed.

Publishing Credits

Contributing Author
Deborah Buchanan

Content Consultant
Blane Conklin, Ph.D.

Associate Editor
Christina Hill, M.A.

Assistant Editor
Torrey Maloof

Editorial Assistants
Kathryn R. Kiley
Judy Tan

Editorial Director
Emily R. Smith, M.A.Ed.

Editor-in-Chief
Sharon Coan, M.S.Ed.

Editorial Manager
Gisela Lee, M.A.

Creative Director
Lee Aucoin

Cover Designer
Lesley Palmer

Designers
Deb Brown
Zac Calbert
Amy Couch
Robin Erickson
Neri Garcia

Publisher
Rachelle Cracchiolo, M.S.Ed.

Teacher Created Materials
5301 Oceanus Drive
Huntington Beach, CA 92649-1030
http://www.tcmpub.com
ISBN 978-0-7439-0433-9

Table of Contents

The Birth of a Leader

Julius Caesar (SEE-zuhr) was an important leader in history. He lived in ancient Rome. Rome was founded around 753 B.C. At first, kings ruled Rome. Romans became unhappy. They threw their last king out of Rome.

The people set up a **republic** around 509 B.C. This meant that men were chosen to rule. Leaders did not have to be born into a royal family. They were chosen by the people. The Roman Republic was a success for a long time. It lasted almost 500 years.

▼ The ruins of ancient Rome are still visited by people today.

Julius Caesar was a major figure in the Roman Republic. His role in the republic changed history forever.

Julius Caesar ▶

Who Gave Rome Its Name?

A famous legend describes how Rome got its name. Romulus (RAWM-yuh-luhs) and Remus (REE-muhs) were brothers. They were raised by a wolf. They decided to each build parts of the same city. They fought over the sizes of their parts. Romulus killed his brother. He became king of the whole city. He named the city Rome after himself.

▼ Romulus and Remus with their wolf mother

Caesar's Social Class

Julius Caesar was born in 100 B.C. His family was neither rich nor poor. He grew up in a simple home in Rome. His father died when Caesar was 16 years old.

Caesar's family belonged to the Julian clan. This was a very old Roman family. They were in a class known as **patricians** (puh-TRIH-shuhnz). However, by the time he was a boy, Caesar's family had lost most of its money. So, Caesar did not grow up in a fancy house or a rich neighborhood.

Many people lived in ancient Rome. However, they were not all equal. They were divided into three social classes. These were citizens, noncitizens, and **slaves**.

Citizens had rights that noncitizens did not. Citizens could own property. And, they could also vote. The citizens could be part of the Roman government. Many laws were unfair for the noncitizens and slaves. And there was nothing they could do about it.

◀ This toga is similar to one that Caesar might have worn.

▲ Most patricians lived in expensive homes like this one.

▼ These women are plebeians.

What's in a Name?

The citizens were called patricians, and they were usually rich. The noncitizens were called **plebeians** (plih-BEE-uhnz). These people were workers, farmers, and soldiers.

Wearing the Toga

At age 16, Caesar was given his first **toga** in a family ceremony. The toga showed that he had reached manhood. Unfortunately, this is also the year that Caesar's father died. He remained close to his mother for many years. She taught him to be very proud and strong.

City and Rural Life

When Caesar was 19, he fell in love with a girl named Cornelia. They were married and had a daughter named Julia. Over the years Caesar rose to power. He was elected to become Roman High Priest. That position had honor, but he did not have much power.

Caesar lived with his family in Rome. Rome was an amazing city. There were beautiful statues and buildings. However, the city was also noisy, dirty, and dangerous. Many Romans lived in small houses with lots of people. The buildings were run down. Sometimes they collapsed.

Some Romans wanted to avoid the city. They lived in the country. The wealthiest Romans also owned **villas** (VIL-luhz) outside of town.

▼ The Roman Forum

▲ Grapes were grown on vines like these.

Country farms produced everything a family needed. This included fruits and vegetables, milk, cheese, wine, and meat. Farmers relied on slaves to help with the crops.

Forum

One of the most famous areas of Rome was the Forum. This was the political center of Rome. Today, tourists can visit the Forum. There, they can stand among the ruins of this great city.

Mosaic Tiles

Mosaics were very popular in ancient Rome. They were made from different colored tiles. The tiles were small pieces of glass, stone, or clay. The artists used the tiles to form patterns or images. Mosaics discovered from long ago give us pictures of Roman life.

◀ Mosaic floor pattern

Roman Gods and Goddesses

Early Romans worshipped gods of nature. They made **sacrifices** (SAK-ruh-fice-ez) to keep the gods happy. The Romans believed that the gods controlled the harvests and weather. Actually, they thought the gods controlled every part of their lives.

The Romans believed in many gods. But, there were three who were the most important gods. Jupiter was the sky god. He was the most powerful god. Juno, his wife, was the goddess of women. Their daughter, Minerva, was the goddess of wisdom. The Romans worshipped these and other gods at festivals. They built temples in their honor.

◀ Minerva was a very brave warrior.

The Pantheon still attracts visitors today. ▶

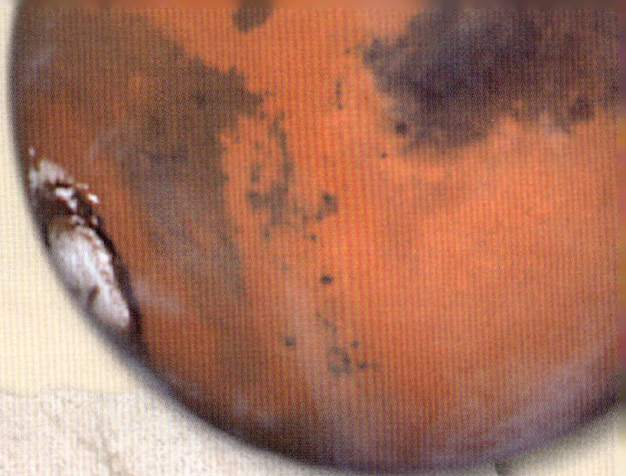

Mars ▶

Caesar's aunt was married to a man named Gaius Marius (GUY-uhs MER-ee-uhs). Marius was a very powerful man in Rome. He helped Caesar to get a job as a priest of Jupiter. This was an important job for Caesar.

Naming the Moons

Many moons and stars are named after Roman gods. Planet names, such as Jupiter and Mars, are also taken from names of gods.

The Pantheon

The Pantheon (PAN-thee-awn) was built between A.D. 118 and 125. It was a temple dedicated to the gods. It has been in use ever since it was built.

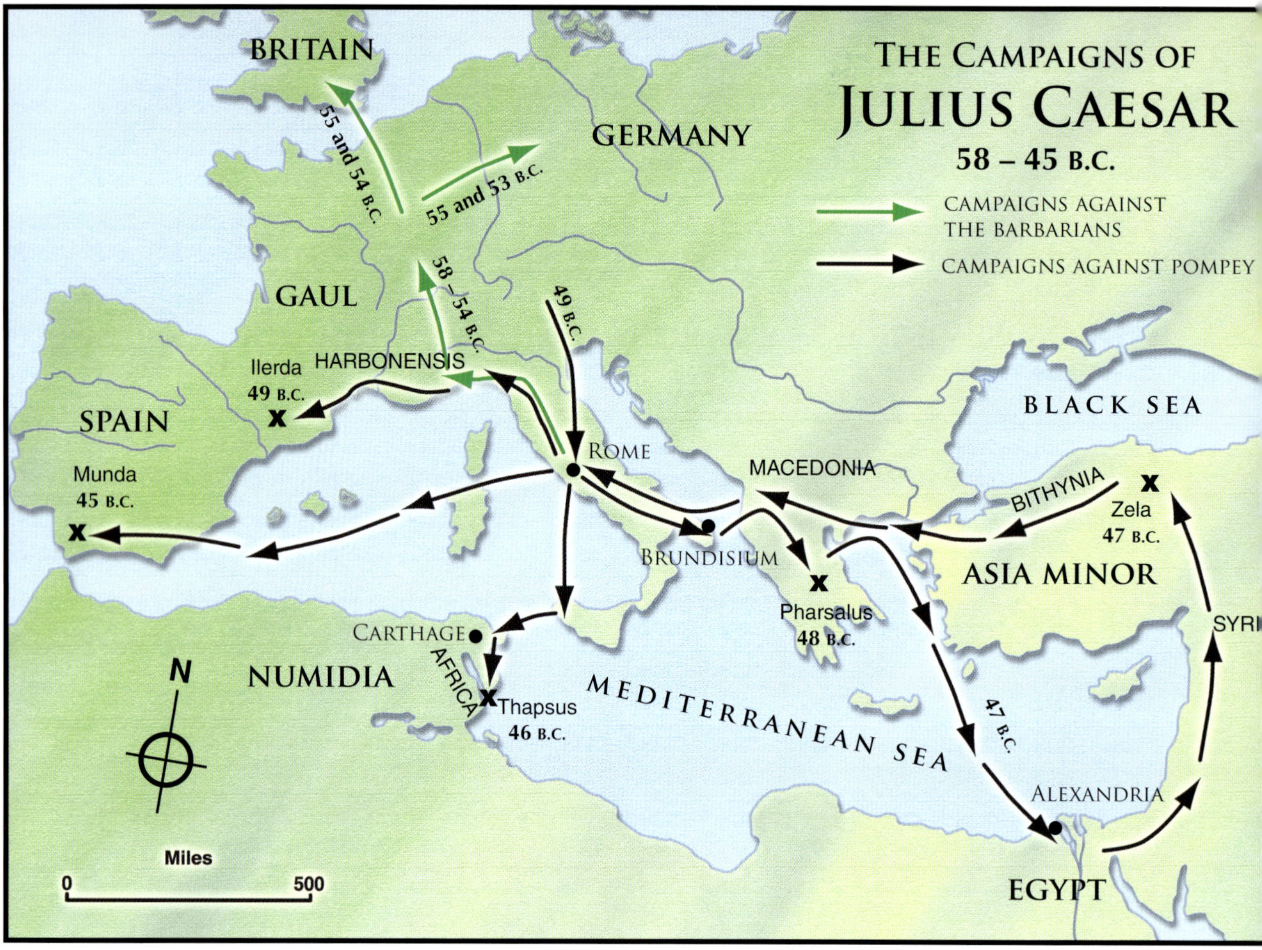

A Talented Military Man

Most boys of Caesar's social class did not go to school. They usually had tutors. Caesar did, too. His tutor taught him about Greek and Roman culture. He also learned to read and write Latin very well. This helped Caesar be a good public speaker.

Caesar was not a very strong boy. But, with a lot of practice, he became a good swimmer, runner, swordsman, and horseman. He also liked to use his mind. All of these skills would help him later in life as a soldier and statesman.

Caesar joined the army at a young age. He quickly became a talented leader. Caesar was very popular. The troops respected him. He saw a lot of success in the military. People started to pay attention to him. He fought and won many battles for Rome.

One important battle took place in Gaul (GAWL). Gaul was where southern France is today. The Roman Republic wanted to rule over Gaul. This would make their republic bigger and stronger. So, the Roman army moved into the area. Caesar won the important battles.

Calendar Creator

The old Roman calendar was very confusing, and it did not work! It was based on **lunar** months. Lunar months last about 28 days. Caesar asked some astronomers to make a new calendar. The new calendar had 365 days a year, plus one extra day in February every fourth year. This new calendar was called the Julian calendar, after Caesar's family.

◄ Caesar earned the respect and trust of Rome's soldiers.

A Powerful Army

Many believe the Roman army was the strongest in history. Julius Caesar was one of the army's most powerful leaders. Early in his career, Caesar risked his life for a fellow soldier who had fallen. For this act of bravery, he was awarded the Civic Crown. He was very proud of this award.

The army was so strong because of the foot soldiers. They were called **legionnaires** (lee-juh-NEARZ). These foot soldiers fought so that the republic would be powerful. Each legion had about 5,000 foot soldiers. They volunteered to join the army.

The legionnaires were strong and brave. They had to be because Rome was always at war. There were many battles for them to fight. Sometimes, the men spent years away from home.

Roman road ▼

The army took good care of its soldiers. They were given weapons such as swords and daggers. They also wore heavy armor and helmets. This protected them from injury or death. The army had many people who traveled with the soldiers. These people took good care of the legionnaires.

All Roads Lead to Rome

Armies needed good roads to march on. So, the Romans built many roads. They wanted the army to travel quickly. The roads were built very strong. Some are still used today.

Shielding Each Other

Legionnaires carried special shields into battle. These were called scutums (SKOO-tuhmz). The shield curved around a soldier's body to protect him. Sometimes, they held all their scutums together to form a huge shield overhead. It was like a turtle's back. So, they called it a tortoise formation.

▼ The Roman army was very powerful.

▲ Julius Caesar as dictator

The Republic Falls

The Roman Republic was in trouble. The elected officials were called the Senate. They argued a lot. And, they did not agree on laws. Many of the Senate members wanted more power.

Rome's citizens had no power in the republic at all. So, some citizens revolted. They wanted the Senate to change.

Caesar, Marcus Crassus (KRAS-uhs), and Pompey the Great took power over Rome together. They called their union a **triumvirate** (try-UHM-vuh-ruht). Over time, the triumvirate fell apart. Crassus died in a battle in 53 B.C. After that, Caesar and Pompey fought for power.

Caesar and his army marched on Rome. Pompey fled.

Shortly after Caesar took control, he decided to make himself a **dictator**. This meant that he would be the only ruler of Rome. This decision would be a turning point in Roman history.

United States Senate

The United States also has a Senate. Americans elect senators, much like the Roman citizens did. In Rome, there were as many as 600 senators at one time. In the United States, there are only 100.

Strong Republics

Many countries today are republics. This means the people choose who they want to lead their country. Elections are held, and people vote for their leaders.

◄ This is the building where the Roman Senate met.

A Betrayal

When Caesar made himself dictator, some people were upset. They felt that Caesar was acting too much like a king. Romans did not want a king in charge of their lives.

Caesar became a great threat to leaders in the Senate. They were worried he would make too many changes for Rome. These men liked keeping the control in the Senate. They did not want Caesar to become too powerful. Some members of the Senate decided to kill Caesar.

▼ Marcus Brutus plotted against Caesar.

Two of Caesar's old friends led the group. They were named Marcus Brutus and Gaius Cassius (GUY-uhs KAS-ee-uhs). Caesar was stabbed to death by a group of senators. He died in 44 B.C.

▼ Caesar is killed by a group of senators.

The Ides of March

Caesar was killed on a day know as the Ides of March. It was the 15th day of the Roman month *Martius*.

Shakespeare Writes

A man named William Shakespeare wrote plays in the 1600s. One of the most memorable moments in his work is Caesar's death. The reader is shocked that Caesar's friends would kill him. This must have been how the people of Rome felt. Over 2,050 years later, that surprising moment in history is still studied.

The Empire Is Born

After Caesar's death, many people were very angry. The Roman middle and lower classes had respected Caesar. They were upset that other leaders had killed him.

Three men took control of Rome after Caesar died. One was Octavian (awk-TAY-vee-uhn). He was Caesar's adopted son. Another was Mark Antony. He was a very popular Roman general. The third man is not as well-known in history. His name was Marcus Lepidus (LEP-uh-duhs). He was a general and had supported Caesar.

◀ Octavian

These men worked together. They defeated Brutus and Cassius. Octavian, Antony, and Lepidus ruled Rome together for many years.

At first, they worked together. But they soon realized that only one man could rule Rome. Octavian won that battle. The Roman Republic was over.

In 27 B.C., Octavian became Rome's first emperor. He was given the name Augustus (oh-GUHS-tuhs). This word means *great*. The Roman Empire had begun.

◀ Mark Antony speaks over Caesar's dead body.

Caesar's Own Words

Julius Caesar was a general and a leader. But, he was also an author. He wrote several texts during his lifetime. Most were about events of the day. Sadly, many of his books have been lost.

Egyptian Queen

Antony was married to Octavian's sister. But, when he left Rome, he fell in love with the Egyptian queen, Cleopatra (klee-uh-PAH-truh). They had several children. Octavian was very angry at Antony for leaving his sister. Cleopatra and Antony died during a battle with Octavian. Antony was not the first Roman who loved Cleopatra. Earlier in her life, Cleopatra and Caesar had a son.

▲ The Trevi Fountain in Rome is a popular tourist sight.

Arches and Domes

The Romans were excellent builders. They copied some styles from ancient Greece. For example, they used arches and columns. But, the Romans had new ideas, too. They were the first to use a dome on a building. The dome on the Pantheon is one of the largest in the world. Some of their incredible buildings are still standing today.

Rome had a great water system. Plumbing helped send fresh water to houses and bathhouses. There were also public fountains. Many people used the water from the fountains in their homes.

Water was important to Romans. Rome can be a very hot place. Fresh water helped keep people cool. It also helped keep people clean. This is very important in a city. Romans often built towns near rivers or springs. They wanted a constant supply of fresh water.

▼ The Arch of Constantine is an example of Roman architecture.

Carrying Water

The Romans invented **aqueducts** (AK-wuh-duhkts). These are pipes or channels that carry water from place to place. They are built above or below ground. Aqueducts help cities get enough water. Many of the aqueducts are still standing today throughout Europe.

Concrete Mixtures

Romans were the first to use concrete. This is a mixture of sand, gravel, cement, and water. It is still used in most modern buildings and roads.

The Latin Language

Most people in early Rome spoke Latin. Different forms of Latin were used. Everyday speech was one form. A more formal Latin was used in literature. Official documents were also written in formal Latin.

Romans learned Latin grammar in school. They also learned to write in Latin. Some students learned Greek, too.

Latin is still used today. Medical and legal terms are often Latin words. Latin is also used to **classify** and name plants and animals. However, Latin is rarely spoken today.

Many modern languages are still influenced by Latin. Latin words or word parts form many English words.

▼ Latin engraved in stone.

Latin Root	English Meaning	English Example
ami	like, love	amiable
cept	take, hold	intercept
dict	tell	dictate
junct	join	junction
mov	move	immovable
ped	foot	centipede
scrib	write	describe
spect	look	spectator
tract	draw, pull	tractor
vid	see	video

Church Services

Catholic church services used to be said in Latin. Then, the church leaders realized that no one could understand what was being said. Today, the services are spoken in the language of the people.

Shared Alphabets

The English alphabet is based on the Latin alphabet. However, there were only 21 letters in the Latin alphabet. The letter *i* was used for both *i* and *j*. The letter *v* was used for *v*, *u*, and *w*. The letters y and z were added to the English alphabet later.

Entertainment in Rome

Romans enjoyed races and games. A popular sport was **chariot** (CHAIR-ee-uht) racing. Races were held in stadiums. Thousands of people came to watch. Chariots were usually pulled by two or four horses. Sometimes, they even used elephants or camels.

Gladiator (GLAD-ee-ay-tuhr) games were also very popular. Men fought against animals and each other. Many fought to their deaths.

▼ The Colosseum is a popular tourist sight.

▲ Chariot racing was very dangerous.

Thousands of people watched the bloody battles. The Colosseum (kawl-uh-SEE-uhm) in Rome was the most famous location for this sport.

Acting was also an important pastime. Roman plays were based on those from ancient Greece. Successful actors were popular like movie stars are today.

Sea Battle

The Colosseum was an amazing place. It was as big as football stadiums are today. They even flooded the floor of the Colosseum to hold huge naval battles. Visitors can go to the building today and see where these events took place.

Gladiator Heroes

Gladiators were the sports stars of the day. Some of them became rich and famous. People all over Rome knew who they were.

◀ This artifact shows two gladiators fighting.

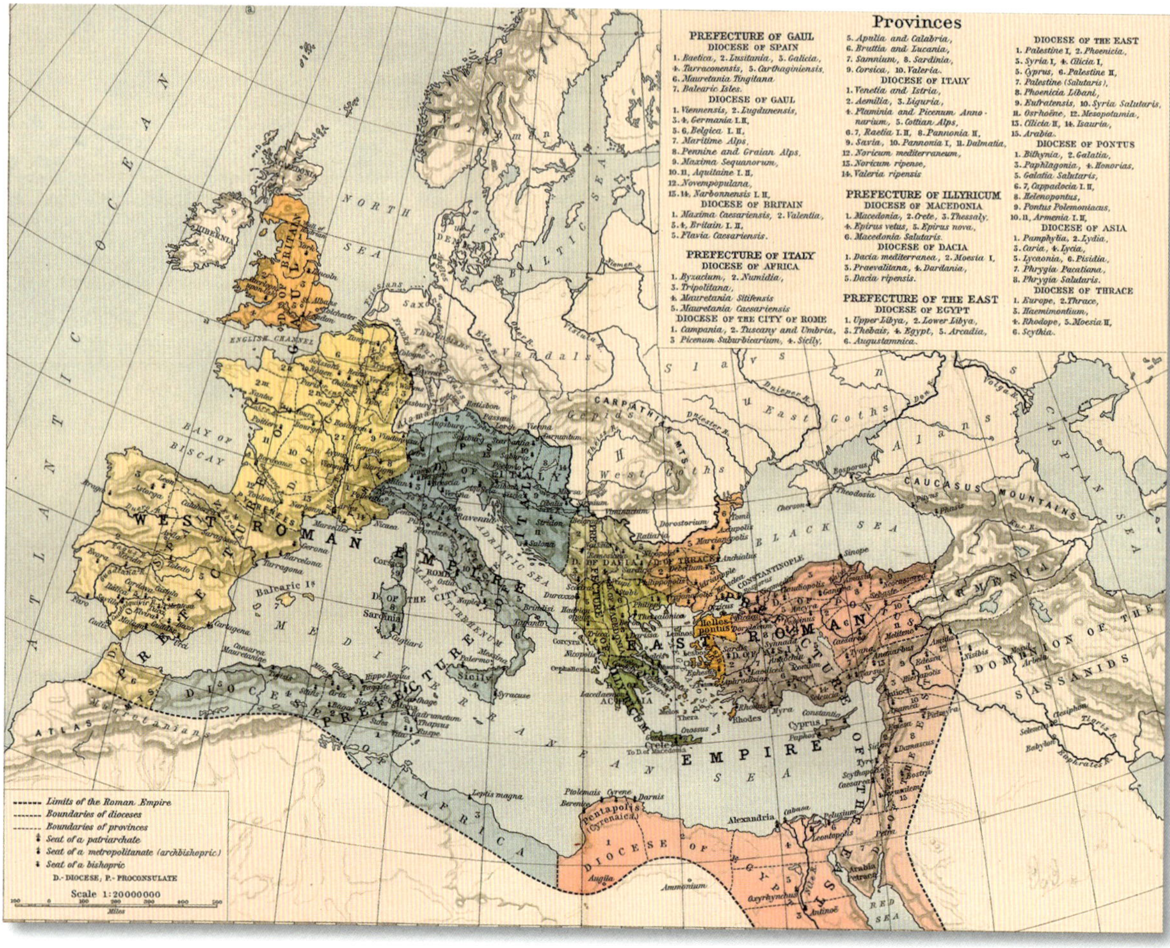

The End of an Empire

Many men ruled over Rome after Julius Caesar. Augustus is famous for being the first emperor of Rome. He worked hard to strengthen the empire. He was a good emperor who took care of Rome.

Not all emperors were as successful. A few of the emperors actually went crazy while they were in control.

The carving is from the Peace Arch, which celebrates the *Pax Romana*.

The Roman Empire came to an end in A.D. 476. How did such a powerful empire fail? Its large size made it difficult to **govern**. Also, the long borders made it easy for enemies to attack.

Ancient Romans continue to impact the world in many ways. Their **legacy** (LEG-uh-see) proves how strong and powerful they once were.

The European Union has special money called the Euro.

Augustus's Peace

Augustus was the first emperor during the *Pax Romana* (PAWKS row-MAWN-ah). That means the *Roman Peace*. This 200-year period was a time of peace for Rome. A lot of progress was made in art and architecture during this time.

The European Union

Today, countries in Europe make up the European Union. It is not one nation like the Roman Empire. But, the countries do work together. They want unity among the different nations.

GLOSSARY

aqueducts—pipes or channels that carry water

chariot—two-wheeled horse-drawn vehicles that participate in races

classify—to arrange or assign to classes

dictator—someone who has total control of a country

gladiator—a person engaged in a fight, often to the death, for public entertainment

govern—to rule or exercise authority over

legacy—something people today have learned from long ago

legionnaires—foot soldiers of the Roman army

lunar—related to the cycles of the moon

patricians—citizens of Rome; the wealthy class

plebeians—noncitizens of Rome; the working class

republic—a country whose rulers are elected by the people

sacrifices—gifts offered to the gods

slaves—people who are owned by others and have no personal rights

toga—a loose outer garment worn in public by ancient Romans

triumvirate—government of three officials ruling together

villas—large country homes

INDEX

Image Credits

cover The Granger Collection, New York; p.1 The Granger Collection, New York; pp.4–5 The Library of Congress; p.5 (left) Heather L. Jones/ Shutterstock, Inc.; p.5 (right) Book Matrix; p.6 Corel; p.7 (top) The Granger Collection, New York; p.7 (bottom) Corel; p.8 The Library of Congress; p.9 (top) Olga Vasilkova/Shutterstock, Inc.; p.9 (bottom) Silvio Fiore/Superstock; p.10 Zastavkin/Shutterstock, Inc; p.11 (top) National Aeronautics and Space Administration; p.11 (bottom) Corel; p.12 Teacher Created Materials; p.13 The Granger Collection, New York; p.14 Photos.com; p.15 The Granger Collection, New York; p.16 Photos.com; p.17 (left) Vanni Archive/Corbis; p.17 (right) VisualField/Shutterstock, Inc.; p.18 The Granger Collection, New York; pp.18–19 SuperStock, Inc.; p.20 The Granger Collection, New York; pp.20–21 The Bridgeman Art Library/Getty Images; pp.22–23 (top) Jenny Solomon/ Shutterstock, Inc.; p.22-23 (bottom) Pierdelune/Shutterstock, Inc.; p.23 Photos. com; p.24 Doug McKinlay/Getty Images; p.25 Stanislav Khrapov/Shutterstock, Inc.; p.26 Corel; p.27 (top) The Granger Collection, New York; p.27 (bottom) The Granger Collection, New York; pp.28–29 The Historical Atlas by William R. Shepherd, 1911; p.29 (top) The Granger Collection, New York; p.29 (bottom) Murat Baysan/Shutterstock, Inc.; back cover The Library of Congress